The Mom Comedies: Do Dragonflies Roar?

Lauren Lauterwasser

ISBN: 0-6155-7771-7
ISBN-13: 9780615577715
LCCN: 2011945194
Do Dragonflies Roar?
Kissimmee, FL

Dedication

This book is dedicated to Anna and Emma, who provide daily inspiration and perspective. I am thoroughly entertained by everything you do, and will continue to enjoy discovering things about life together. You win everything else, but I win the I Love Yous.

Acknowledgements

Tim, thank you for making daily life so enjoyable. I married the man you were, and I'm very lucky to share my life with the wonderful father and true partner that you've become. I've had the time of my life creating these memories with you.

———— ◆ ————

Mom, you opened a whole new world when you took me to the library on a rainy day. Your love, encouragement, patience, advice and sense of humor have shaped who I am.

———— ◆ ————

Dad, I am glad that you were never satisfied with "The tree is green," and coached me to bring my homework assignments alive with descriptive phrases. These exercises in imagination and perspective provided the foundation that made me want to write.

———— ◆ ————

Mom & Dad Lauterwasser, thanks for making me your fifth child. Your support, encouragement, and love mean more than you will ever know.

———— ◆ ————

Marcella, Mike, Katrina and Jared: I enjoy dwelling in this village that is raising our children. Having six in three years makes us experts, and I am fascinated to watch this litter of children continue to develop. Your stories, reassurances, recommendations, honesty and sense of humor are a never-ending source of support. Marcella, thank you for always being there for me, no matter what.

———

Michelle & Christine, you have made the girls trendy. The things you have taught them make for some of the best stories (and videos!). Look for them to storm Manhattan in the near future, as this will likely provide fodder for Book Two.

———

To all those who encouraged me to produce this collection, and those who read the multiple drafts: this book would not be here without you. Aunt Tina and Aunt Sally, your whispered encouragement continues to inspire me. Thank you all for helping me to realize my potential.

———

.

The Inspiration and Cast of Characters

The word "hobby" has a peaceful connotation. It conjures images of someone exercising mind, body, or soul. Before having children, my hobbies included cooking, reading, and other euphemisms for depleting my disposable income.

Now I truly have no hobbies. Any time that I have to exercise my mind, body, or soul is fraught with guilt at the stuff I'm not doing instead. If I read or try to do ten minutes of yoga, my mind is distracted by the basket of unfolded laundry in the next room. Other household chores are frequently interrupted by protecting the children from each other, dousing flames in a random part of the house, or refereeing nonsense arguments. One night my kids threw simultaneous tantrums over an imaginary pink dinosaur. "No—it's MINE!" I pulled another imaginary dinosaur out of thin air, but they didn't like that one. Fighting continued over the single imaginary creature. I left them to sort it out and went to get wine.

I found that writing about the ridiculousness was fun and therapeutic. As I continued to share my thoughts on public forums, the reaction I got from others indicated that this insanity is mimicked daily in households across America. I found comfort and confidence in the laughter and camaraderie and decided to assemble the stories as a collection. Now you can feel normal, too!

You'll notice that the stories become much shorter as time progresses; this is a direct result of the amount of time I have to write. Before having children I had loads of time to pontificate; now I am grateful for smart phones where I can jot down six or seven words as a reminder before the memory floats away.

The cast of characters in our carnival includes Tim (husband), Anna (currently a five-year-old), Emma (currently a three-year-old), and Mackensie (a very patient dog). Other characters (including grandparents, The Armadillo, The Muslims, The Stripper, and The Biggest Bug Ever) will be introduced as necessary throughout this occasionally chronological story, which begins at the point Tim and I began unexpectedly expanding our family.

Pregnancy: A Brief Synopsis of Good and Evil

Definitely the best part of pregnancy is the cravings. I never, ever expected them to be so much fun. Although mine weren't tremendously exotic (can't crave oysters if you've never had 'em), they arrived fast and furious. You've likely heard the frugal advice "Don't grocery shop when you're hungry." Well, I have news for you—the best way to save money during pregnancy is to keep the woman out of the grocery store and throw out anything remotely resembling a menu (including *The Yellow Pages* with its glorious restaurant guide). When I would return from a two-hour grocery store excursion, Tim would find himself alarmed as he carried in six bags of canned peaches, several boxes of chocolate-covered cherries, multiple gallons of ice cream, and a dozen frozen pizzas, in addition to our more standard items like milk and chicken. I don't know if he was concerned about money or space, but pregnant grocery shopping will eat up both.

On the flip side, there was a not-fun part, especially for Tim. I did not enjoy the hormone swings of my teenage years and early twenties, and I had made great strides in attempting to be "logical" about my emotions. I figured that this would carry over naturally into my pregnancy (cue laugh track). The mood swings were so violent that there was no warning for me or any other unfortunate soul who happened to be within shouting distance. I used to smile politely and spend a few minutes speaking with the Jehovah's Witnesses who accosted me outside the grocery store; suddenly, even the Girl Scouts peddling their delicious cookies weren't safe. I believe that the word "hormonicidal" should be added to the dictionary to describe the mood swings of pregnant women.

———————

The New Parent's Shopping List

Tim and I were among the first of our friends to have a child. We went through the obligatory "deer in the headlights" phase when registering for baby items. I liked picking bath toys and bibs; I cried when it came to selecting a breast pump and a stroller. I liked the stroller that had pink paisley fabric and was all set to add it to our registry when Tim starting saying something sensible about price and size and weight and safety ratings.

He said, "Here, see if you can pick this up."

I said, "Why? It's pretty. I'm ready to do something else. What this baby REALLY needs is a milkshake. Come find me when you're done test driving this thing."

So what advice did we give fellow new parents? I'd have to say that a video monitor was one of the most indispensable items for the first few years. Is the child standing up or lying down? Are they climbing out? Did the pacifier fall out of the crib? The video monitor allows you to be neurotic without letting the child know. However I frequently wished that, in addition to sight and sound, the monitor would provide a long-distance smelling mechanism. I never knew if they were standing up because they'd filled their diaper.

A close second in the must-have category is a dog. As much as I'd have liked to keep the high chair sitting on a disposable tarp, it just didn't go with the rest of the décor. Once dinner was done, Tim would hose off the baby and I would clean up the table and go find the dog to act as a very enthusiastic vacuum.

Before we had children, we bought a king-size bed to accommodate our two spoiled dogs. The upgrade turned out to be a smart buy because it eventually had to accommodate two kids as well. The kids profess to be scared of the dark yet cross approximately 500 square feet of pitch black space in order to stand over us and declare that we are having a sleepover. One night after getting kicked and smacked too many times, I grumpily stalked to the couch and found Tim already there, snoring peacefully. I curled up on the love seat and we slept like surprise house guests while the giant cozy bed was crowded with our offspring.

———

Maternity Clothes

Some part of me honestly thought ("hoped" is probably a better word) that I wouldn't need maternity clothes until the ninth month of pregnancy. I can't even offer an explanation for that except maybe "delusion." My Mom was on a crusade to put me in maternity clothes immediately, so that I didn't somehow "crush" this peanut-sized object with deadly items like jeans and tank tops.

The first item of discussion (or "battle") was underwear. My mother wanted me to get granny panties, an idea that I immediately vetoed. I told her that my belly was pregnant, not my rear end; she countered that I needed to start acting like a Mom and wearing the underwear to match. In a pinch they can be used as a t-shirt since they pretty much run from thigh to collarbone. It does get better as the belly starts expanding, and the collarbone line starts to inch back down to its normal space in the navel region. My veto was successful.

I didn't really have much choice for style in the remaining items. In most of the shirts, there's some shape in the collar and then it just drifts down like a teepee, with no contour whatsoever. However as your stomach pushes out you are grateful for the extended length, so the belly doesn't hang out. The pattern choices are limited and, if you shop online like I did, most things you might consider wearing are out of stock (probably because creating these huge clothes results in fabric shortages worldwide).

To sum it up in a phrase, maternity clothes are kind of goofy-looking. But they are so comfortable. I wish all clothes were that comfortable with no zippers, snaps, or buttons. But when the time came I was very happy to get back to my normal wardrobe!

Childbirth Preparation Class

Before our first child was born, we attended an all-day childbirth preparation class. This included childcare instructions and the Lamaze breathing technique and was informative, fun, and a little scary. We had a great crowd of eight couples who seemed equally freaked out.

The class was taught by a wonderful woman who had sixteen years of experience as a nurse in the delivery room and two kids of her own. Her personality was very calm and comforting as she described, in graphic detail, what would occur during labor and delivery. As squeamish as I am, I would much rather know what is coming than be surprised. Despite the overall success of the class, I had a few moments of sheer terror.

The uneasiness started when our teacher described the water breaking. I determined that I simply needed to start wearing Depends during the last few weeks of labor to accommodate the two pounds of amniotic fluid that my body would suddenly decide it didn't need anymore. Even tsunamis are preceded by an earthquake warning—women get nothing (although one could argue that we should just be on the lookout).

Tim was relatively unfazed by this information; he determined that he would merely sleep in his bathing suit.

The panic truly started to set in when we were shown a dilation size chart. The magic number for pushing is 10 cm. I never really had a concept of the true size of 10 cm until she held up the stages of dilation chart. You've likely heard the analogy of delivering a watermelon or a bowling ball…that's because both of those things can fit through the 10 cm opening. I could wear a 10-cm hat. It was at this point that I started fanning myself with diaper coupons.

I was ready for the pain, but I really wasn't interested in experiencing ALL the science of the delivery. Hence I was very grateful that our instructor warned us about the placenta.

She held up this massive web of netting and cord and said, "This is your placenta. Doctors will usually want to show you this miracle of how your baby has been kept alive inside you. If you don't want to see it, make sure you tell him or her."

Luckily the instructor had smelling salts with her—after I woke up, I told Tim that he would get a divorce and the doctor a swift kick in the chin if I caught any sight of the placenta.

Tim said, "Hey, cool—you're going to have a baby AND a jellyfish."

I got my bearings after several hours of more normal discussions, such as what to expect after the baby gets home. We also watched the "Bill Cosby, Himself" skit about natural childbirth…we'd both seen it so often we could recite right along with Bill, but boy was it more meaningful given our new perspectives.

Then Teach brought out her suitcase full of torture devices. I felt like I was at a French Revolution museum: "This is a catheter...This is the epidural line...This is a vacuum..." They all started to get fuzzy after a while.

I felt like I had in high school when we had to dissect a frog. Anxious about the task at hand, I was relieved at the time to have a partner who seemed interested in performing the dissection (now she's a doctor and I'm still writing essays). Ten years later I was getting another science overload; fortunately, once again I had a calm partner and didn't have to see any of the stuff that made me woozy.

Baby Brain

My apologies to the women reading this, however I must admit something before proceeding: women have occasional moments of sheer stupidity (boys—you're welcome). At times, this is endearing and works in our favor because it makes the big strong men think that we couldn't possibly stay alive for more than two weeks without them to guide us through life, so they should probably marry and keep us safe. As an example, have any of you women ever put the milk away in a cabinet, and the cereal in the refrigerator? Even for thirty seconds, before you smack yourself on the head and pray no one saw you? I may have skewed minor details, but I bet most of you girls are snickering silently at yourselves right now.

Don't worry, you don't have to confess your silly moments to anyone but yourself, because you can usually bury these random occasions of idiocy. When you're pregnant, you might as well take out an ad on the front page of a newspaper and announce, "Don't trust me by myself for nine months."

Compounding the ridiculousness of your actions is your hormones causing you to completely overreact. One night I put dinner in the oven and promptly forgot about it. When Tim opened the oven and said, "Ooh, chicken jerky!" I was inconsolable for hours. The staff of a grocery store searched for my debit card before I sheepishly realized that I had put it in my back pocket for easy access. And that was before I looked pregnant, so I couldn't use the expanding belly as a crutch to explain my idiocy. I flew into a murderous rage upon realizing that baking soda and baking powder are not interchangeable when making a cake.

"Bed rest" is a civil way to keep insanely foolish women locked up for nine months so they don't do further damage.

License to Parent

As my third trimester approached and I lost the ability to put on my own socks, I considered the monumental task I had in front of me. Beyond labor and delivery, I suddenly realized that we would be responsible for taking a helpless little baby and turning it into an articulate, clean, well-adjusted, well-mannered member of society. Just a *tad* intimidating. I felt like I had jumped out of a plane with the parachute unattached to my terrified self.

Tim and I were relatively normal, educated, middle-class individuals. We should therefore be able to handle this absurd duty, despite my overwhelming fears. I mean, if it was that difficult, the government would issue a license for it...right? If I want to operate any kind of vehicle—boat, plane, tractor-trailer, motorcycle, automobile—there's a different license for each of these. (In Florida, I can even choose to ride a motorcycle without a helmet...but I'll get my license taken away if I ride in a car without a seatbelt.)

Tim needs a license to sit out on a boat all day and drop dental floss into the water hoping to wrestle into the boat something that he can buy easily in the store. Hunters all over the country need to carry their licenses to overpower frightening animals like deer and ducks.

The woman who does my pedicure needs to display her license with a picture in a frame so I have something to look at when she tickles my feet.

So I would think that the job of bringing another whole person into the world would require the most extreme licensing process. But you only need to go to the local "Crowded Germy Trampoline" for a birthday party to discover people who clearly would not meet the standards for licensure.

Lamaze is only a half-hearted attempt at physical training. They teach you how to breathe, an involuntary function at which most of us excel since we've made it this far. Even if the mom fails the class, she can still deliver the baby and raise the child. How do I change a diaper? Give a bath? Cut those little nails? Not injure the soft spot? Keep the head from rolling off the shoulders?

My mother told me that if a baby cries, it needs one of three things: a burp, a diaper, or food. She said we were lucky, since she had to worry about whether diaper pins were sticking her children. She also told a rather inspiring story that gave me the wonderful gift of perspective. When I was a child, I could not drink regular milk. The doctor told my mom that she needed to buy goat's milk for me to drink. After scouring the town, my mom found the lone pharmacy that sold goat's milk for an astronomical fee per case. Undeterred, she went home and told my father that he needed to buy a goat. I try to achieve this same confidence in my own parenting decisions.

The short "baby care" class discussed previously covers the very basic things (excluding goats). It's not mandatory. There is no final exam. No degree I can hang proudly in my living room that says, "I've Been Trained to Raise a Child." I definitely would have felt more prepared if there were a grad school for parenting. But you take the advice of those who have gone before you. Search for the parents who have four kids and are still reasonably pleasant and then if you find any, make sure to ask them for anxiety medication recommendations in addition to parenting tips.

Nesting

I'd like to know the name of the psychologist (probably male) who coined the term "nesting." For me, this conjures an image of a destitute pigeon gathering trash and twigs because it can't go to the store and get a crib.

Like most things in pregnancy, I had a preconceived notion of what to expect from this concept. Once I forced the pigeon image out of my head, I was able to come up with a much nicer, wholesome representation: an apron and a skirt, with a feather duster (very "June Cleaver"). The element I wasn't anticipating was the dementia that took over and highlighted my normal obsessive tendencies.

Dusting, rearranging, polishing, scrubbing…I had to regrettably evict the family of dust bunnies that had cemented themselves to the top of our kitchen cabinets. Yes, I said "top of our kitchen cabinets." Picture Tim's face when I asked for the ladder. "No, not that one—the BIG ladder." I can't put into words the psychosis that overtook me—the best I can do is provide an example of the simple act of turning on a light (so I could see better under the refrigerator). Something wiggled when I hit the light switch, and damn if there wasn't a loose screw on the switch plate. Out came the flat-head screwdriver, as my hormones drove me around the house, frantically tightening all the switch plates. Then I noticed a screw on a doorknob—it wasn't loose, but I figured why not check the rest of the doors in the house.

This will sound crazy to everyone but women who've had a baby: the thought actually crossed my mind about bulldozing the house and building from scratch. I wouldn't hire anyone to do this (I wouldn't even let Tim in on it) because if I didn't do it myself then it wasn't done right!

"The Point"

Women should be allowed to hibernate during the last 6 weeks of pregnancy. It's rather tiring all by itself, especially because we must mentally prepare for the physical ordeal ahead of us that will end this whole process. The insomnia gets a little annoying after a while… that's why we nest, because we find ourselves curiously awake in the middle of the night, wondering what to do with ourselves. May as well be productive and go iron every article of clothing in the house.

By the time the sun comes up and it's time to go to work, we need a nap and stare listlessly into the closet… those once-enormous maternity clothes are now too snug. It's not practical to go buy bigger maternity clothes because there are only a few weeks left…so you're left putting ridiculous layers of lotion on your legs just to grease the sides of the pants. And the pants that go all the way over the belly are the only option at this point, because every tent/shirt will get caught in the pocket that has been created between the top of the belly and the bottom of the "chest area." Once the clothes have been put on, go search for shoes that fit on those Fred Flintstone feet. It's a great bonus if they actually match the outfit and are not flip-flops or tennis shoes.

A reminder to you that Fred Flintstone feet exist because your body starts retaining massive quantities of water. Everything swells—rings don't fit, shoes don't fit, socks leave a ring around what was once an ankle, faces look like marshmallows with lips, and as one of my friends said, "I woke up and realized that even my nose had gained weight."

You'd think that with the body making sausages out of everything, the water would be redirected and this would reduce the urge to pee. Cruelly, this is not the case. It's not a matter of your body eliminating waste productively…it's just that you can't possibly get everything out at one shot. The baby is sitting on the tiny pipe that leads from the bladder to the exit valve, which means that when you have to go…you just don't. Interesting acrobatics occur in the bathroom as you attempt to bend or straighten your body into a position that will allow the pipe to properly empty the bladder.

This gets more interesting at the doctor's office when you have to pee in a cup. As described, it's hard to pee anyway, but your belly has become so big that you can no longer see the cup. Baby brain prevents you from remembering this, so during each office visit you almost have to do a somersault before remembering that you just have to trust that you will blindly find the target.

Birthing Children

So far, my husband and I have demonstrated absolutely no skill at family planning. Like most women before me, I was petrified of childbirth. By the time I got to the ninth month, I had a working theory that evolution has made human gestation slightly longer than necessary. During this extra few days or weeks of unnecessary pregnancy, the mother/host becomes so delirious with bloat and fatigue and tents-for-clothes that she does not care how the baby is removed from the body.

My thirty-hour labor was not unique. Nor, I suspect, was my offer of a cash reward to the epidural technician. After the pain disappeared, I noted that my body had grown some extra appendages: a blood pressure cuff, an IV, a urine catheter, and the epidural catheter. Then someone said something about sticking a monitor on the baby's head which, from my perspective, was still inaccessible.

I stopped watching and muttered to my husband, "Can you please make a list of all the things that are connected to me? The least you can do after putting me in this predicament is to make sure all this stuff comes out."

Then came the fateful moment: I slid to the end of the table and human stirrups came to hold my legs. The doctor told me to push and I suddenly realized that I had no idea what that meant. So I held my breath and made a face that I hoped made it look like I was pushing. The doc told me I was doing great and making progress.

When I told her I had been faking it, she said, "You're moving along. You want a mirror?"

So the words I yelled in the delivery room were not at Tim, but to the delivery staff: "NO MIRRORS!"

I finally sorta figured out what to do. It sucked, and then it was over. I felt something being pulled out of me, and a flurry of activity started. Tim cut the cord, and then they whisked the baby over to some sort of counter where they washed it and weighed it and put powder on its feet. They looked like they were preparing a turkey. Everyone followed the baby and left me on the bed. No more human stirrups, no more encouragement, no more attention.

I asked, "Can someone at least remove my catheter? And what do I do with this placenta?"

The doc took pity on me and came over to put all my organs back in, or remove them, or whatever happens.

I said, "Is it a girl?"

Nodding slightly, she said, "Yep. As advertised."

The next ten months are a bit of a blur because I spent every second in shock. And then we got pregnant again.

I'm always a little sheepish when I tell people I'm pregnant. You can say something cute like "We're expecting" or "There's a bun in the oven" or (my favorite) "I need a leave of absence in about ten months." But I feel like the hidden message every time is "Heeey, guess what? My husband and I had sex! And it WORKED!"

Warnings about the Early Days of Parenthood

The early days of Anna's life were among the most traumatic of my rather boring life. I remember wondering why no one warned me about certain things, so I'm assembling a list for all those soon-to-be-parents or those who are considering this path in life.

1. The hospital will force you to ask for hints about how to change a diaper. They provide all the proper tools like diapers and washcloths and cream, but you're left on your own to assemble this strange jigsaw puzzle. Luckily Tim had way more logic than I did and chastised me for calling the nurse for a tutorial. But it's best to make sure that at least one parent has practiced this activity. Practicing on a doll is not realistic. Borrow a small, hyper dog and make sure that rehearsal includes a bleary-eyed, middle-of-the-night changing.

2.   The hospital will wisely not allow new parents to leave until competency with a car seat is demonstrated. Beyond this, there is no instruction booklet for the child. (When I bought a blender, it was accompanied by a manual in English, Spanish, and French, along with a DVD.) Once the child is buckled in, they send you on your merry way with a free diaper bag and some formula samples. This trend is alarming.

3.   You really don't get any sleep for a while. It's not pleasant. Buy lots of eye cream and strong coffee. Don't make any hasty decisions for the first several weeks, like giving the child up for adoption or getting a divorce. You will never again look with disdain upon a hotel that rents rooms by the hour where you can hide and take a nap.

4.   An awful lot of things can be done with one arm. However, if evolution continues then I believe people would spontaneously generate a third arm upon becoming parents.

5.   You become surprisingly efficient. If you hear the baby waking up and know that you have five to seven minutes until he or she starts getting fussy, you will be able to make the bed, empty the dishwasher, throw in a load

of laundry, take a shower, and have three gulps of the extra-strong coffee before having to entertain the kid and change a diaper.

6. You start to intensely dislike your pets and their simple demands. You sigh loudly when you have to feed them or walk them. "What do you mean you need another walk? You had one yesterday." And they become so darn CLINGY. Mackensie was a normal healthy dog before Anna was born and then suddenly had three paws in the grave with all her illnesses. Be prepared for the pets to take a back seat.

7. Babies really do say *goo goo*. I always thought that was some weak representation of baby cooing, kind of like *bow wow* or *woof woof* for dog barking. But they really do say *goo*, and it is the cutest sound in the world.

Babysitting

It's wonderful having available babysitters you can trust…namely grandparents.

These people have raised you and presumably done an adequate job. Yet when you drop off *your* kid, it's as if you are attempting to describe how to operate a nuclear reactor. There is no conversation, only endless babble by the new parents directed at the grandparents who are half listening and mostly making faces at the baby who couldn't care less that its parents are going bye-bye for an hour.

"We are going to Chili's. Here is the phone number. Do you have our cell phone numbers? My cell phone is fully charged, but I brought the charger just in case. We picked Chili's because it's close—if your phone stops working you can just walk to get us. She was fed at 5:30 and got a new diaper at 5:15. She will probably want to eat again around 7:30 and she usually goes to sleep around this time. Hold her with your right arm against the wall at a ninety-degree angle and under her knees with your left hand under her head and support her neck while you rub her back. Here, lemme draw a picture. Make sure it's dark and quiet and do a lazy walk so you bounce her a little bit. If she's not tired, don't force her to go to sleep. Sometimes she likes to bang the pacifier over your left eye—just let her go because this will get her tired, too."

And this goes on for ten minutes. The new parents will call twice before they get to the restaurant, which is an eighth of a mile away. Dinner will be eaten in a hurry and on the edge of the seat so that maximum cell phone reception is achieved.

When you are finished dinner and you're driving to pick up the baby, you will wish you'd eaten slower and enjoyed the time away a bit more. You brace yourself to walk in and find haggard grandparents and a crying child and are somewhat impressed to walk in and find a snoring baby and calm grandparents. You drive home and wish you didn't have heartburn.

Middle of the Night Fun

At some point, new parents realize they must stop attending to every middle of the night cry. Training a baby to put itself to sleep is another exercise in anxiety, patience, and compromise.

During out first attempt at this, Tim and I had discussions and made promises that were so emphatic you'd have thought we were planning a battle against a well-armed enemy. We looked into each other's eyes and firmly resolved that we would simply go in and let her know we were there, but only by standing above the crib without rocking her back to sleep. After about 90 minutes, Anna was still wide-eyed and giggling at us. She wasn't crying or upset, just maddeningly awake.

At about the time she was starting to drift off to sleep, Daddy's foot kicked a stuffed toy at the foot of her crib. It cheerfully announced, "Baby Bear needs a hug." Tim grabbed the talking toy and departed to remove its batteries or light it on fire; I never was sure how that one turned out. In the end, we broke down and picked her up, and she fell fast asleep after about a minute.

Future attempts at this involved us huddled outside her door, clutching each other while we wondered whether at what point we were supposed to succumb to the awful pressure and just go walk her around. I had determined that thirty minutes of rocking her to sleep every night was better than two or three ten-minute episodes of listening to her cry it out. Like most things in parenting, it passes quickly and you forget all about it until you have the next child. And years later, you will ache for one more chance to rock your baby to sleep.

———— ◆ ————

Going Back to Work

Leaving your newborn to rejoin the working world makes pregnancy and labor look like a breeze. There is suddenly no task or job that seems as important as caring for the drooling, incontinent, adorable blob that is about to be left with strangers. After having my first-born, I had to repeatedly tell myself that earning money towards her school tuition, toys, and clothes (not to mention electricity) is an equally beneficial way to provide for her.

Like every Mom, I had done a lot of hard thinking about what I could do to stay home with her. The ideas ranged from the plausible ("I could sell my car, which would eliminate the payment, the insurance, the gas, and the tolls…. that's a whole paycheck!") to the ridiculous ("We would have hot water every night for dinner. Maybe add some raisins for flavor, but only on the first Sunday of every month.").

It was as though I was heading over a cliff and clutching at anything that happened to be protruding from the edge. It was during the last few weeks of maternity leave that I actually started to give some serious thought to assembling the arcane collection of stories that you're currently reading. Anything to earn a paycheck yet stay home!

But I did return to the working world, kicking and screaming all the while. Since I was nursing, the task of pumping provided a tremendous distraction. While I was committed to the method of feeding I had chosen, there was nothing that caused me greater anxiety than having to watch the clock during meetings and try to furtively sneak into an empty office, rig up the pump system, and attempt to relax. The building that I worked in at the time had a tin roof and the offices had no ceilings; if it was a quiet day, you could clearly hear the rhythmic sound of the pump. I used to kick the wall and slam drawers just to create background noise.

Getting the milk home was no picnic either. Since it needed to be refrigerated, it was always the first priority as soon as I walked in the door. Pour it into bags, label the date, stuff it into the freezer, clean the parts—I was in the house for 30 minutes before I could do anything else, to include spending quality time with the baby. It's all truly exhausting and a bit depressing, but doesn't last forever.

When the Mobile Milk Machine days are over, the challenges don't go away. You might think your lightning transition from Parent to Employee is complete, until you stand up and announce to your co-workers that you have to "go potty." Likewise, you discover your true friends are when they point out the dinosaur sticker adhered to your butt, or the spit-up trailing down the back of your clothes.

Changing a Diaper on a Plane

New parents can be comically cautious about changing a diaper in public, despite the presence of those convenient but germy changing tables. Throw that caution to the wind once you've changed a diaper on a plane. It's kinda like bungee jumping if you're scared of heights—once you face the fear in the worst possible situation, the fear is overcome.

Picture yourself squeezing down the narrow center corridor of the plane with a squirming six-month-old and a diaper bag. Anna attempted to grab the hair of someone in every third row, and the diaper bag bumped the heads of those she missed.

The beverage cart attendant smiled sweetly and said, "I'll move in just a moment, sweetie. Now sir, what can I get you? We have coffee, tea, Coke, Diet Coke, Sprite, Diet Sprite, Ginger Ale, orange soda, orange juice, apple juice, tomato juice, wine, domestic and imported beer, assorted cocktails…" This went on for as long as it took Anna to attack the magazine of the innocent bystander in the seat next to us (she was unsuccessful in ruining it, thanks to Mom's acrobatics).

Now enter the bathroom. It's difficult enough to drop your own drawers in the kitchen-cabinet-sized space…add a diaper bag and attempt to keep the fidgety kid from touching every imaginable toxic surface and I was more than ready to go back and request one of those assorted cocktails from the flight attendant. At least there was a changing table.

As soon as I was undoing Anna's old diaper, we heard a beep. Anna picked her head up to find out what was beeping, just as the plane lost a half mile of altitude. "Ladies and gentlemen, please return immediately to your seats and fasten your seat belts. We are in for a bumpy few minutes." Despite the changing table, there was no harness to keep Wiggle Worm in place. She bumped her head at one point and started audibly complaining, and I prayed for those spontaneously generated third and fourth arms.

After a while, we made it out alive and relatively unharmed, despite our unkempt appearances (Anna's pants were on backwards and her unbuttoned onesie gave her a curious tail). As I marched back down the aisle, oblivious to the heads we were bumping, we ran into the beverage cart lady again. I got the same sweet smile along with the obligatory "I'll move in just a moment, hon. Now sir, what can I get you? We have coffee, tea—"

"Move" was my only word. I think the expression on my face said the rest as she slid out of the way.

Circus Act

"Anna...*Anna*! Touch your nose!! Yaaay!! Now touch your ear...Anna, Anna look at me...*touch your ear*!!!! Hooray!!! Anna, how big? Anna, stop crying. Anna, why are you running away from me? No, sit *down* we have to do patty cake!!"

The firstborn becomes your very own roaming circus act. We would go out and ask Anna to do tricks as if she was a dog, and as if the people watching truly cared. She started to look at us as if to say, "My ear has not moved since the last time you asked me." She touched her nose so often that she started to realize that fingers and nostrils have rather complementary shapes, and would get sidetracked wondering what to do when her finger got lodged in her nose.

So by this point the children are endlessly entertaining and sleeping through the night. Now parental instinct kicks in, amnesia suddenly occurs, and having another child is discussed. Consider yourself warned.

The Parent Olympics

Friends and co-workers talk at length about the latest fads in exercise. Some promote variations in exercises to "trick" the muscles, and this lack of routine results in hard-bodied, smiling (and, oddly, glistening) individuals who are finally content with themselves.

I have my own rigorous workout program with variations in exercise. There is also little choice involved in the particular "reps" that occur.

For example, I carry a twenty-five-pound wriggling weight all around the grocery store, while simultaneously pushing a full cart with another child. I see other participants engaging in similar activities. I feel a bit self-conscious next to the mom with four kids and two carts, but I'll work up to that advanced level someday.

After a brief rest, I may do "step runs." For example, while putting Emma down for a nap, she might request a variety of misplaced stuffed animals, all of which are downstairs. Since she asks for three animals, one at a time, I am able to complete a nice set. I am so lucky to have my family support me and push me further.

There should be a Parent Olympics for this type of specialized exercise. "Laundry Basket Pushing" would involve entertaining multiple children at once. Victory goes to the parent who reaches the finish line first without capsizing the basket or otherwise injuring the children. Fans of Curling could get their fix watching parents with a mop trying to keep kids off the wet floor. On further thought, I'm starting to think that maybe this would make a better sitcom/game show.

Enough daydreaming—I must get back to training.

Baby Toys

Parents get to exercise their powers of logic and patience with baby toys. They come in packaging designed to survive a direct bomb hit. It is therefore necessary to stay up all night removing the product from the packaging before showing it to the baby who wants to play with it immediately. Extracting the toy from its prison usually requires two adults, a screwdriver, a pair of scissors, and a closet full of batteries. Incidentally, I'm confident that changing the packaging on children's toys could significantly increase the life expectancy of the planet.

Once the product is set free, Mom and Dad want to take it for a spin so they can show the baby how to use it. Dad will proudly show off all of the toy's capabilities to Mom, and Mom may or may not be impressed with how much Daddy knows about colors and nursery rhymes. The baby will gaze upon the toy Into which money and time have been invested and play with it for five minutes before wanting to be entertained by the next thing. Unless the parents can stir up a parade in the living room, it is necessary to have at least a hundred toys on hand at any given time in order to keep the baby occupied.

Really, the toys are unnecessary since infants find almost everything to be fascinating. Anna would find microscopic pieces of lint or flaws in the tile and scratch at them for hours. I lost three leg freckles to that pudgy finger. Paper towel rolls, measuring spoons, egg dividers—the random household objects create the most fun, although parents tend to ignore this for toys that have been evaluated by some obscure committee of experts.

And the toys do have benefits. For instance, children will learn how to "push" rather quickly, since many of the toys will talk or play music when the child depresses its mid-section. They concentrate very hard, get that little fist ready, and *push*…then laugh and clap when the desired reaction is achieved. When they find your belly button, you will feel obligated to sing a song every time the child pokes it.

In the never-ending quest to stimulate Anna as a toddler, I cleared Wal-Mart of all the toys marked "Six Months and Up." One of these items was a tiny little bongo that promised to teach the baby numbers, letters, and music. They only had one of these left on the shelf and the batteries were dead so I couldn't test it in the store. Two months later, I finally replaced the batteries and gave it to her.

When I turned it on, I heard, *"Escucha!"* I looked for the button to switch the toy from Spanish to English…and it was nowhere to be found. Meanwhile, Anna thinks this is the best toy she's ever seen and proceeds to pound on the bongo that is encouraging her by shouting, *"Fantastico!"* Despite the packaging and the directions being English, *Toca de Tambor* was indeed a Spanish-only toy.

I have never lived down that episode. Tim has his own moments, for which he is unapologetic. Anna had a mobile with farm animals. I tirelessly imitated each farm animal sound, but one day I caught Tim describing the tastiness of each animal.

Shocked, I said, "Cows say *moo!*"

He calmly overruled me. "No, cows say *sizzle.*"

As the children get older, toy assembly for Christmas becomes far more complicated because it must be done in hiding. Trying to put together a dollhouse in a closet requires more patience than I am capable of producing, so Tim assembles anything that has more than a paragraph of instructions.

One Christmas, Tim was absolutely buried with work, so I valiantly tried to take over some of his construction duties. I started with something simple: the box advertised "7 pieces" although the component identifier went all the way to the Letter Z. Clearly I was set up for failure from the beginning. I kept my grumbling to a minimum, but needed to ask questions such as, "Is the hammer fully charged?" and "Why don't they give you screws that fit?" He patted my head, told me I was pretty, and threatened my life if I ever went near the tools again.

Mistaken Identity

Humans over the age of three can understand simple reasoning; for instance, an object is not necessarily a car just because it has wheels. However, early cognitive development is critical for realizing that subtle distinctions can be very important when classifying items into their proper categories. The first time I put on the movie *E.T.*, Anna cheered and asked if he was the *real* Wall-E. I didn't know how to defend my answer, so I offered a vague response, "He sure looks like him!"

Other lessons are accompanied by paralyzing social awkwardness. We took the kids for a bike ride one night around Christmas time and passed a Muslim family playing baseball in the street. The mother came out of the house wearing a blue burka and Anna shouted, "Hey look, there's Mary!" Mortified, we hoped that the family would assume that Mary was the name of Anna's teacher or perhaps a distant relative on our adopted cousin's side. Alas, our hopes were dashed when the husband came out. "And there's Joseph!"

Likewise, Emma has learned that dreadlocks on men are common. At a doctor's office, she was very excited to meet Bob Marley. "Bob" was not from Jamaica (nor was he dead), but he was a very good sport about letting Emma think she'd met one of her favorite singers.

Hidden Messages

Parents make a lot of decisions that solve short-term problems and then become anxious later when they wonder if they're developing the appropriate "foundation" of thought for their kids. For instance, I don't particularly want my children to turn into alcoholics; however, when my they are sick, I give them bright liquid in a miniature shot glass and say, "Here. This will make you feel better."

And how do we teach our kids to ignore peer pressure, the staple of youth? It's certainly not by uttering this daily prophecy: "Your sister eats all of HER cereal. She's going to be big and strong. Don't you want to be big and strong, too?" The bandwagon marketing strategy comes naturally to parents. Then later we'll ask them if they would jump off a bridge just because their friend did. Isn't this what we've taught them?

I used to think it was cute when people described thunder and lightning in imaginary terms to children, but I wondered why they didn't just explain the science. I understand now, especially when it is 3:00 a.m. and the bed is crowded with children who are scared of thunder and suddenly curious about why the outside is blinking. Faced with the task of explaining the mechanics of electricity and sound, it's so much more appealing to explain it instead as those fun-loving angels out bowling at all hours of the night.

——— ———

The Farmers

Gardening played an important role in the up-bringing of both my husband and me. He retained his patience for, and interest in, growth, dirt, and bugs, while I outgrew it sometime around my fourth birthday. However, watching a child plant seeds is one of life's special moments, which I spoil with grumblings of, "Don't let her get dirty—I'm not ready for baths."

During planting season, Anna and Emma call each other "farmers" and like to tell stories about how the seeds will turn into a fruit/vegetable/flower. One day, Emma pulled a tiny opaque ball out of the dirt. When Tim told her it was a lizard egg, Emma slowly put it back in the planter. For weeks, we waited for her to tell people that she was growing cucumbers, corn, and lizards.

The summer is a busy time at my job, so Tim and the girls would stay in south New Jersey with Tim's family during that time. While driving me to the airport so I could fly back to work, Tim would half-heartedly acknowledge my sadness at leaving the family and then skip to detailed instructions for how to care for the garden in his absence. Instructions included sending pictures of the tomato plants and telling me to pick any crops that were "ready." How was I supposed to know what met that requirement? Food was ready when the timer went off.

His children had similar priorities. When I would go back to New Jersey after a week at work, I always took a late flight. I'd climb into the bed between the girls and relish the thought of them waking up to see that Momma was back. When the time came, I awoke to find Anna grinning from ear to ear, her nose touching mine.

She asked, "Were you at home? How tall are the corn plants?"

The Botany Experience knew no boundaries. One morning I went in search of Tim after irritably attempting to single-handedly complete the school-and-work preparation routine. I found him outside using a paintbrush on a zucchini plant. He explained sixth-grade science to me: apparently he was playing the role of the bee by helping to pollinate the plant. I silently watched this dispassionate creation of life wondering if I should play Barry White or pour some wine. I slowly retreated when the kids wandered outside to ask what he was doing.

English, the Foreign Language

I was born and raised in the Northeast, outside of Philadelphia. We have our own vernacular and accents, but I consider most of our expressions to be pretty normal. Although I've lived in Florida for almost fifteen years, I still do double-takes when I hear certain Southern gems. For instance, "There's more than one way to skin a cat." Really? What are the options? And how did this phrase gain popularity over other contenders? There are a number of alternatives that can convey Southern charm without violence. I'd like to propose "There's more than one way to fix the tractor" or perhaps "There's a bunch of ways to slop the hogs." Even violence can be conveyed with a more recognizable analogy: "There's more than one way to slaughter a cow."

Further evidence of cruelty against felines is demonstrated when Southerners indicate quantity by stating, "You couldn't swing a dead cat without hitting (random object)." The visual is alarming, but the clarification through the use of the word "dead" is what intrigues me the most. Does this make the expression more convincing, as opposed to swinging a sleeping kitty?

Observing the development of a toddler's speech cortex is a fascinating process in itself, presenting unique challenges in communication and frequent moments of hilarity. Learning syllable progression can be especially challenging.

"Emma, it's HULA HOOP. Say HULA HOOP."

"Hoop-a-loop."

"No. HU-LA HOOP."

"HULA poop."

It was Emma who would also command me to fetch her bathing soup when she wanted to go swimming.

After overhearing me say that Emma could sleep through a war, Anna told her cousin, "My sister sleeps like a worm." We didn't correct her that time and made no effort to clarify when she would proudly point at pictures of our wedding and say, "That's when Mommy and Daddy got buried."

I had a real-life Abbott & Costello moment with Anna while trying to reinforce the concepts of left and right.

Anna held up her left hand and asked, "Is this left?"

Like a dope I said, "RIGHT! Wait, no, it's left, but it's correct."

Confused, she held up her right hand and said, "Then is this left?"

"Ask your father," I said.

I've had a hearing loss since birth and wear hearing aids. I also have less than perfect eyesight; hence, I have earned the nickname Four Eyes and Four Ears from my loving husband. After I watched him struggle to understand something that our then two-year-old was saying, I was thrilled to realize that I finally had the perfect example to convey my own hearing process. You really catch only every third syllable and then you have to try to process this information to form a logical interpretation of what is being said. This process can be a fabulous tantrum starter, since a child's patience quickly runs thin. I spent an entire night bewildered by the following conversation I'd had with Emma:

"Mommy, I want…any M's."

"Um…we don't have any M's. Do you want to buy a vowel?"

"NOOOOOO…I JUST WANT ANY M'S! MY CHOCOLATE!"

"Oh, M&M candy?"

"Yes. M for Emma."

———

The Armadillo

Tim and I have had a variety of pets over the years: several dogs, the obligatory fish, a bunny rabbit, and an iguana. The iguana was purchased by my husband while we were in college, and she stuck around for a long time. We always got the same appalled fascination from new-comers to our house: "What is that? A dinosaur?" We referred to her as our green dog.

During our iguana's last days with us, a wayward armadillo wandered into our backyard and decided to audition as our next "weird pet." Initially Tim complained, but I could see a tiny gleam of excitement in his eye. He came out one morning holding a pitchfork and announced he was going to "gig" for armadillos.

Apparently, armadillos have evolved enough to avoid gigging. So Tim, in all his *Homo sapiens* glory, rigged a sophisticated trap of bamboo and a cast net. Our armadillo possessed above-average intelligence, so the trap did not work. Tim furiously began pricing cross-bows on eBay. I patiently suggested that he drive his car around the backyard and that the armadillo would in-stinctively run in front of it.

The hunter bought the crossbow. I marveled at the confidence he had in his archery skills since the kill zone is pretty small on an animal born with armor (plus Tim had never shot an arrow in his life).

Late one night, Tim left to walk the dog. I had a heart attack as the front door flew open and a tall blur streaked past me, yelling something incoherent. Panicked and trailing after him, I feared that someone was trying to break into the house. As I contemplated dialing 911, Tim raced back outside carrying the cast net. Realization dawned, so I grabbed my camera and ran after him.

Apparently, the dog had trotted up the walk and encountered the armadillo. Each of the two animals went along its merry way as the hunter ran to get his trusty net. Of course by the time Tim got back outside, the armadillo was long gone. Frustrated, he blamed Mackensie, our friendly thirteen-year-old, twelve-pound Maltese.

"How could she just let it walk right by?"

I told him his expectations were a little high; granted, Mackensie still had about four teeth, but I don't think any of them would strike a death blow to an armadillo.

The week progressed and the trap grew even more elaborate. I was actually pretty impressed with the ingenuity of the design. However, it remained empty.

A few nights later, déjà vu struck as I was walking to bed and the blur ran by. The cast net was replaced by the more effective "large Rubbermaid container." He called after me to get a cinderblock, but I was carrying the camera so I ignored him. I was there to be entertained, not help.

Breathe easy—the cinderblock was to weigh down the Rubbermaid container, not squish the armadillo. Once the armadillo was safely captive in its bubble, Tim gathered the regulation armadillo trapping supplies: heavy-duty gloves, a pet carrier and…a baby gate? I bet him ten dollars he couldn't get the damn thing into the pet carrier, but I lost.

I will only admit that the armadillo survived but never again entered our backyard.

When my family attended Thanksgiving dinner the following week, everyone looked suspiciously at the turkey. I had to assure them that it was poultry and not something else.

Hibernating in Summer

I somehow ended up living in Florida despite growing up outside of Philadelphia and being a homebody. During the first few years, the summers were unbearable and I spent as little time as possible outside. The tolerance for weather is like a law of nature—as heat tolerance increases, tolerance for cold decreases. Although I don't have to shovel or put chains on my tires, I do have to put sunscreen on myself and loved ones before going to get the mail or put the trash out. At least the snowy states get pleasant experiences like fireplaces—although, we do get to enjoy the smell of smoke because half of Florida is on fire at any given time during the summer.

Floridians tend to hibernate in the summer. While the rest of the country heads to Disney World, we've sequestered ourselves in a cold location. We shut the blinds, leave the house only in emergencies, and long for more pleasant weather, which usually comes around mid-October. We need to get a mascot like Punxsutawney Phil who will see his shadow and tell us if there will be six more weeks of summer. Okeechobee Otto would be a terrific name for an armadillo mascot, although armadillos tend to be slow to react to shadows (even when accompanied by a blaring car horn).

The Biggest Bug Ever

Adrenaline is a fascinating conditioned response that compels the body to react in life-threatening situations. For instance: when a four-inch palmetto bug crawls out from under a rug in a small bathroom occupied by a mother and her cubs. Adrenaline will cause the mother to shout "EEK!" and search frantically for a shotgun while simultaneously throwing her children to safety out on the roof. There is nothing removable in the bathroom heavier than a bottle of shampoo, so it's decision time about whether to follow the monster or find a murder weapon. I curse myself for being such a neat freak and not leaving shoes and hammers strewn about wherever they fall and grab the first hard-bound book I see.

Armed to the teeth with a book of nursery rhymes, I stalk the prey. He is hiding on a stuffed animal, but upon seeing me, he makes a break for the dollhouse. I don't actually catch him over open carpet because I suddenly feel faint imagining what sound a bug that size would make upon being squished. While dealing with wooziness, I determine that perhaps Tim is better at pest destruction; however, he is working downstairs in the office. I have visions of my warrior husband blindfolded, spearing The Bug with his crossbow, and the merciless teasing I would suffer afterwards.

Sensing my weakness, The Bug runs right for me with the intention of having a tasty meal. I give a battle cry and bring the book crashing down. I pick it up and he limps onward, his antennae mocking me with their victory dance.

More yelling and seven more blows end his reign of terror. As I wipe blood from my brow and console the girls, Tim comes up spluttering something about a cave-in of the ceiling.

"Next time, just call me before you destroy something in addition to the bug."

Aching with battle fatigue, I manage a smile and realize that I should have tried this strategy years ago.

The Beach

When I was young, my family's annual vacation was always at the Walt Disney World Resort in Florida. We'd pile in the car with suitcases and enough entertainment for the twenty-hour drive, stop at every Shoney's on Interstate 95, and anxiously await the sighting of the first palm tree. I have innumerable happy memories of our vacations there, although none of them include a trip to the beach.

Upon meeting my husband's family, they promptly offered to host me at their shore house in Avalon, NJ. However before I had children, I strongly disliked spending a day at the beach. I couldn't figure out why since I find the sound of the ocean soothing and I cannot fathom living more than a few hours away from the ocean. Plus I really loved beach towns. I eventually determined why it's not my favorite: the combination of sunscreen and sand makes me feel like a breaded chicken.

Of course, after having children I couldn't avoid going to the beach, and I grew to actually like spending a day in the sand. (This is probably because it provides endless entertainment to my children, while I enjoy a margarita smuggled past the dunes in a yogurt cup.) But preparing for the daily trek to the waterfront is exhausting. With no fewer than four children and six adults in the house at any time, the logistics are staggering.

The food must be packed, and include healthy snacks, treats, and a case of juice boxes. This will require at least four coolers. An umbrella and tent provide shelter. Towels, beach chairs, and boogie boards are other essentials. Hats, sunglasses, sunscreen and lip balm round out the list of items that will complete the sentence, "Ooh, I forgot _____." And most importantly, a garage full of toys must be transported to the ocean: shovels, rakes, buckets, trucks, sand shape makers, Barbies, and other items you will grow to dislike as you dig them out of the sand eight hours later.

While undertaking this monumental packing effort, don't forget that someone has to get the kids ready. I suspect that putting suntan lotion on a toddler or infant is very similar to wrestling a greased pig. The squealing alone is practically identical.

By the time all this is finished, it is time to begin the day at the beach. We look like nomadic pack mules as we hike the five blocks from the house to the beach with all of the aforementioned items. Setting up camp is a little easier, since the children are now splashing in the ocean and not underfoot.

Despite the exhaustion, it's a lot of fun. It's a simple day free from electronic entertainment, where kids must use their imaginations and nature to have fun.

———

Athletics

I've never been an athlete. When I was a junior in high school I made a fledgling attempt to run track and running three miles is still my life's crowning physical achievement. I proudly purchased new sneakers that year and was dismayed fifteen years later when the sole began to separate from the shoe. I try not to dwell on the fact that humans can travel to space faster than I can run a mile.

My star athlete boyfriend played soccer in his high school and early college career, with track and field as a hobby. Because physical exertion was an alien concept for me, I was fascinated to observe the superstitions that go along with playing a sport—the same "lucky" shirt and pair of socks worn for every game, regardless of their condition. I'd see him run on to the soccer field and jog in place for four steps, always beginning with the left foot. I'd see other team members touch the goal post with a specific sequence of body parts.

Similar habits occur when a favorite sports team is in the playoffs. The Philadelphia Flyers would be losing a key game and Tim would grumble that someone must have washed their underwear or shaved their beard. He would go so far as to wish harm on the other team, which I found to be slightly offensive. I would just hope they'd get vertigo and skate in circles.

As products of twelve years of Catholic school, we really couldn't be blamed for connecting two completely unrelated events. Burying a statue upside down in a garden will help sell a house. Having a one-sided conversation with Saint Anthony will help find a lost item (this has never failed me). Pouring oil and water over something is only considered "cooking" when you're not at a Baptism.

It's good to find comfort in any form, even if it's through illogical cause and effect.

Contrary to the image I portray, I actually do exercise. I just don't do it all at once like most people. At work, it's about eighty-five paces from my desk to the restroom. This means that in one year at work, I can walk the equivalent of three marathons. Slow and steady wins the race. I also enjoy seasonal activities, such as walking with a heavy jacket in the winter and wading through ankle-deep water in the summer.

If I do ever decide to exercise consistently, I will probably go back to running. I am inspired by two strangers whom I saw running the annual Disney Marathon. They were passing through the countries in EPCOT at Walt Disney World when we were there. The two runners stopped during the marathon at the margarita stand in Mexico. They went on their merry way, drinks in hand. That's my kind of exercise!

Inconvenient Technology

Technology has changed our lives in remarkable ways. That's quite an understatement, but there really is no way of conveying this point without a lot of words and examples. There is a lingering misconception that technology will somehow make our lives easier, predominantly by saving time. But human nature prevails, and we refuse to rest on that plateau of relaxation and time savings. We're simply filling the time with more activities—mostly searching for apps that will save us more time to search for more apps.

I'm not a hater. For the most part, I really like technology. It does make my life easier in many ways and demonstrates the ingenuity of the human mind. How'd they come up with touch screens? That's cool stuff!

However, I dislike certain types of technology. I'm advocating the return of simplicity to cell phone voicemail. I do not want to page this person, I do not want to leave a call back number, and I don't want more options! I just want to leave a damn message! And what do I get if I select "more options?" Perhaps the current price of stamps or the weather in Denmark?

Another of my pet peeves is customer service phone prompts that only allow voice response and not keypad input. When there are kids around, you get this feedback from the unsympathetic robot: "I don't understand. Did you say, 'Get that crayon out of your ear?' Let me get you to someone who can help."

And who doesn't like the auto correction that occurs when texting? It ruins any kind of edge I'm attempting to give my words. Words like "shut," "duck," and "add" don't have the same ferocity as their intended counterparts. My favorite texting story occurred when Anna and Emma were around the ages of two years, and six months. They were in the tub and Tim left the house to go grocery shopping. At one point, Anna started trying to climb out of the tub. Her slippery footholds were accompanied by cries of "*lw, iw*!!" I looked down to see the much-feared log-shaped objects floating in the tub next to Emma.

Anna was completely traumatized while Emma obliviously splashed. I got both dripping babies out of the tub, wrapped them in towels, and whisked them off to the other upstairs bathroom, thanking my stars the whole time that there *was* another upstairs bathroom. While I waited for the water to draw, I simultaneously tried to sing a song to a very upset Anna, keep Emma from climbing into the toilet, and frantically text Tim for assistance.

Later, Tim said that the message "Anna popped in the tin, hurry home," came through loud and clear.

I love my latest cell phone. Good thing it comes with GPS, because it frequently disappears into another room while Tim dissects its programming. He says odd things like, "Do you want me to sync your Yahoo email with Gmail and Facebook? So you have one contact for everyone with their picture?" My blank stare earns a frustrated sigh from the Director of Technology, and he compares my intelligence to that of a monkey. I have to disagree; I consider myself particularly evolved because I can read and don't have to use pictures to identify things. I am patient, though, and I do look forward to shopping in the app store—someday.

The Holidays

The turkey was a disaster in *National Lampoon's Christmas Vacation*. But it was pretty unrealistic to cook only one turkey to feed thirteen people. That would never happen in our families where turkeys are roasted, fried, grilled, and smoked and where there is a comfortable three-person-per-turkey ratio. One year the kids were fascinated watching Tim place one of the birds into its brine. He told them he was making turkey punch.

Kids have an uncomplicated list of items for which to express thanks. When she was four, Anna came home from school with an arts and crafts project upon which the teacher had written, "Anna is thankful for paint and airplanes." Emma likewise said she was thankful for underpants. We finally realized that we were needlessly worrying about being creative with their Christmas presents.

One year we found a terrific Christmas tree that was misplaced in the eight-to-nine foot category. It was actually a rather obnoxious ten and a half feet tall. The first morning that Tim watered it, the girls gazed at the tippy top, which would surely have been among the clouds if our house had weather. Emma cautioned Tim, "Don't water it too much, or it'll grow bigger."

One of my life's greatest joys has been to pass on Christmas traditions to our girls. Some of them have sketchy origins ("The pickle in the tree means good luck.") and others are simply fun ("Santa wants six cookies. And a beer."). Christmas Eve visits from Jehovah's Witnesses occur with enough frequency to be considered a tradition.

Last Christmas, two very nice gentlemen stopped by and since I was feeling merry I decided to listen to what they said. I had trouble hearing them over the din created by the girls, who had just received stuffed Rudolph and Clarice reindeer from Santa and insisted on re-enacting the entire show on the front porch. After that was finished, I encouraged our visitors to continue telling me about how natural disasters are punishment from God. Tim wandered out with wet hair, wearing a towel, so we were further distracted. The two men thrust some pamphlets at me and quickly departed.

That same year, when Christmas was over and the decorations were being boxed, Anna asked the whereabouts of our Baby Jesus that had just been "born" in the manger. Tim told her he had to go away to grow up and spread peace, and we would crucify him in late Spring.

Easter tends to be a somewhat half-hearted attempt at a holiday. Prep time is merely a weekend of dying eggs and pouring candy into a basket. The traditions are fun, though—my favorite is when I have to call my mother so she can remind me how to hard-boil the eggs. And even at an early age, our kids demonstrated an understanding of the true meaning of Easter. When Anna was three, all the eggs fell off the drying rack and she said, "JE-sus CHRIST!"

Perspective

It's good practice to associate with individuals whose perspectives are different from your own. We are taught that diversity of thought is ideal on a team, yet we still instinctively shy away from those who see the world differently. Children provide the wonderful gift of different perspectives on a daily basis. They challenge the things we say, as well as the things we don't say. They don't have enough experience to jump to the same conclusions we do.

When Emma was learning colors and body parts, I asked her, "What color are Mommy's eyes?"

After intensely studying what I thought was the iris of my eye, she announced that my eye color was "white."

Later that same year, Emma asked me the whereabouts of her toy Rudolph. I distractedly told her that it was under the TV; although, I made the assumption that she'd look in the cabinet.

I learned that I still had some progress to make regarding articulation when she appeared beside me a few minutes later and asked, "Can you help me pick up the TV?"

I'm a huge fan of coupons. My wonderfully patient grandfather spent his early "married with children" years in the throes of The Depression. Therefore, when he used to take me grocery shopping with him, coupon cutting was a very important part of the process. Early on, I taught the girls that expired coupons represented missed opportunities.

One day Tim told me that I had to relinquish control of our household coupon cutting because I was working a lot of hours. Apparently he and I had different perspectives. When I observed his "new and improved" filing system, I found a batteries coupon in the section for Pastas, Rices, Helpers. I graciously told Tim I'd move the coupon to the Miscellaneous/Other category.

His response: "No, keep it there. Batteries help me."

I splurged and bought myself a treasure at one of my favorite clothing stores: a gray and black striped dress, work appropriate, slimming, and fifty percent off the price. I happily attired myself and then stood before Emma the Fashionista for evaluation.

"Do you like Mommy's new dress?"

With no compassion whatsoever she said, "No. You look like a zebra."

I restrained myself from telling her that her tutu skirt was merely two legwarmers short of a Cyndi Lauper video.

Food

I made scrambled eggs for Emma one morning, and they were still steaming when I placed the breakfast in front of her. "Emma, don't touch them yet. See that smoke? That means they're too hot to eat."

After a few minutes of curious staring, she said, "Um. I don't want to eat smoke."

Most days Tim is the one preparing the eggs. One morning he teased her by saying, "All we have this morning are alligator eggs."

Emma shrieked and demanded "regular eggs."

Testing a theory, Tim said, "Okay…then all we have are chicken eggs."

More shrieking. "I don't want chicken eggs!!"

We stopped the torture at that point and served her "regular eggs."

Weather

One winter we went north, hoping for a snowfall. The snow had not arrived the first night but was forecast for the second day. Before putting Emma to bed, we gazed outside and hoped for snow. We folded our hands and then closed our eyes.

"Emma, let's pray for snow. Jesus, please let it snow tonight." While silence followed, I repeated, "Emma, let's ask Jesus to let it snow tonight." When the silence persisted, I opened one eye to find Emma's forehead stuck to the window.

"Momma," she whispered reverently, "it's not working."

———

Anna has a rough time sorting her natural disasters. During the summer of 2011, the Northeast had a rare earthquake that was quickly followed by a pounding from a hurricane. While we watched the big storm on the satellite, she called her Mom-Mom and Pops to ask, "Is the earthquake there yet? Do you have a lot of wind and rain?"

With those recent events on her mind, Anna asked to watch "The Big Tomato." In response to my bewildered expression, Emma clarified for her sister: "She wants to watch Dorothy and the Wizard."

And on another occasion: "Emma, when there's a big earthquake under the water, you have to watch out for salamis."

So hurricanes are earthquakes, tornadoes are tomatoes, and tsunamis are salamis. I'm guessing we don't have a future meteorologist in the house.

Bugs and Flowers

Emma discovered a dragonfly in our lanai. (If you don't live in Florida, "lanais" are the big screened box-like structures we have over our pools, patios, and backyards to shield us from the bounty of flying, stinging, biting, and buzzing wildlife.) While she hyperventilated, I explained that dragonflies are harmless and won't bite her—or carry her away. She calmed down, and I congratulated myself on my superior nature lesson. But Emma was still thinking.

Eyeing the large insect warily, Emma asked, "Does he roar?"

When kids say that they saw a "little bug," they mean "little" as compared to their three-foot-high selves. As they grow older, I'm sure they'll learn that a six-inch palmetto bug is not so little after all.

———

Anna Rose's pre-K celebrated the end of school with a "spring concert." I bought flowers for her, but of course I couldn't ignore Emma Grace.

After handing Anna the flower, I said, "It's a beautiful rose, just like Anna Rose."

Anna looked at Emma's purple flower and asked, "Is that a Grace?"

———

Miscellaneous Gems

Tim thought he was being discreet when he gave me a pat on the butt as he walked past. Anna made him apologize and promise not to do it again.

The first time we took the kids to eat at Germany in EPCOT, Anna was asked, "Are you German?"
She replied, "No. I'm Anna."

I dislike when a cafeteria serves food (other than ice cream) with an ice cream scoop. Scrambled eggs and pulled pork should not be dished out with a utensil associated with the holiest of desserts.

Our neighbor is outside a lot in his bathing suit, which is perfectly normal. But if he walks the dog in his boxers, I get judgmental. It's pretty much the same outfit, so why does the difference seem so important?

A male acquaintance approached me one day and pointed out his new hearing aid. After I admired its sleek design and body style, he asked me how I handled hearing loss, socially. He was probably looking for sympathy…but I pointed out the positives for him, like new nickname opportunities (Four Ears), a noise cushion when his kids got loud, and an alibi for when his wife asks him to do something ("What? Oh, I didn't hear you.").

He admitted he was depressed, and I pointed to his Mets shirt and said, "The Mets should depress you. This is nothing." After we said our goodbyes, I realized I should give up on the dream of being a counselor.

It is entertaining to watch the adult when a child is being potty-trained: tucking the kid under one arm, shouting encouragement, hurdling impossible obstacles, and skidding around corners to get to the potty. And when the child successfully "goes potty," praise and rewards are heaped on the little one. Shouldn't the parent get some accolades? When a running back scores a touchdown, do we give credit to the football?

Excerpts in Awesomeness (about Tim, named by Tim)

My husband is very skilled at writing, which is unusual for someone who needs some practice in the spelling department. I find this quirk to be completely adorable. One time I overheard him complaining to a friend that he couldn't find foot pedals on eBay. "When I search, I keep getting flowers and stuff." Ah, the pain of homophones.

While I appreciate this foible, it's even more important that I can recognize and interpret when necessary. My abilities in this arena enable us to avoid a nasty fight while on vacation in South New Jersey, where he would frequently wake up in the dead of night to go fishing for the elusive striped bass (referred to as a "striper"). At 4:00 a.m., I was awakened by a text message that said, "I got a stripper!"

When the kids were very young, Tim stayed home with them. He was a phenomenal stay-at-home parent, much better than I would have been. He cooked, cleaned, grocery shopped, did laundry and ironing, and kept the kids happily entertained. I would have feigned daily exhaustion if he were the one working outside the house.

But nothing is without its price. I had to endure fantastic teasing. For instance, if I were looking for something he would tell me that we kept it next to the vacuum. I'd sigh and make a half-hearted attempt to look before finally asking where we kept the vacuum. He never tired of this game and would gleefully move the vacuum just so he could hide things near it.

He also liked to have fun in public, at my expense. On the first day of pre-school, I knelt down to take a picture with the girls…and my front-slit skirt split about another inch higher. Tim LIED to everyone within earshot by announcing, "Oh geez. Of all days for you not to wear underwear."

The children would unintentionally tease him on my behalf. His standard attire from April to October is a bathing suit. When Anna was four, she took off her shirt and walked around in her jeans.

She proudly crowed, "I look like Daddy!"

Whenever he would put on a shirt, Emma would ask, "Where are we going?"

When Anna turned two, her birthday party theme was Nemo. I thought it would be cute to get a goldfish as a decoration (although it's somewhat irresponsible to get a pet as an accessory).

Tim grumbled about cleaning the tank and played his ace card. "What are we going to tell her when it dies?"

I stared at him and said, "Seriously? We can't distract her for a few hours while we round up some spare change and go buy a new one?"

He was ready with his response: "But it won't know any of the tricks she taught the old one."

The fish turned out to be a wise purchase. Anna is extraordinarily suspicious of our efforts to get her to try new food. Despite this, Tim didn't expect her to put up too much of a fight when he made her an individual strawberry shortcake. She wanted nothing to do with the strawberries. Even when they were removed, she didn't believe it was just cake and whipped cream.

However, this didn't deter a very clever daddy. Tim got out a candle, lit it, and stuck it in front of the fish tank. After a rousing rendition of "Happy Birthday, Dear Fishy," Anna ate the shortcake. Another entry in the diaries of parental brilliance.

A Collage of Random Brilliant Tidbits

Tim failed to see the charm in playing "Ring around the Rosie." And he took the fun away for me when he said, "Why are we teaching our child a nursery rhyme about the bubonic plague?"

———————————

When I tried to exit the wrong door at the pediatric dentist, I told the kids, "Mommy has lost her marbles."

The receptionist said, "Oh! We found them!" and retrieved four marbles from a spot on her desk.

Tim said, "Oh no, that's not them. Hers have been missing for years."

———————————

Idea for a new thrill ride: glass-bottomed planes.

———————————

During our first overnight hotel stay without kids, we walked into the room and Tim said, "Oooooooh, top bunk, I call it!"

———————————

Emma scored a goal in family soccer. Tim said, "Way to go, Emma! You're a real Lauterwasser. Not a fake Lauterwasser like Mommy."

———————————

It's so sweet when a Daddy wants to grant his child's every wish. After leaving EPCOT at Walt Disney World, Emma sobbed for more fireworks. Anxious to appease her, Tim promised, "Don't worry, Emma. I'll blow something up when we get home."

One day we got the kids out of the pool due to an approaching storm. We all took a spin through the garden to see the butterflies and then announced it was time to take baths. The kids ran ahead of us, stripped off their bathing suits, and went skinny-dipping. I told Tim, "Oh my God, your children are swimming naked."

"They're not naked," he said. "They have goggles on."

Self-Respect

Like most Moms, I was infinitely more sophisticated and smart before having children. Now I find myself involved in rather interesting conversations and don't care so much about someone's perception of me as I seek clarity to a situation. This is what causes kids to think their parents are slow and dumb. My brain used to process things at lightning speed, and now I have discussions such as the following:

Tim: "Quick—go put that T-O-Y away."

Me: "Wait, what? Start over again. Go slow this time."

I keep up the charade of being smart and sophisticated by going to work every day. Attired in clothes free from peanut butter and markers, I try to do a good job and occasionally have something smart to say. I pride myself in fooling everyone…except the kids. Once when I was doing work at home, Anna caught sight of my spreadsheet. She asked what I was doing, and I told her I was working.

"You puttin' numbers in the rectangles?" My attempts to make it sound more important were uninspired. I had to take the gridlines off my spreadsheets to get that innocent insult out of my head.

Sometimes they don't let me off that easy and give me visible trauma that forces me to discuss it with others. After a long weekend, I carefully applied makeup to the giant bruise above my eye. I was correct in my assumption that Human Resources had never heard the explanation, "I got beaned in the head with a harmonica by a toddler singing 'I Got You Babe.'"

These are the things that distract me when my mother instant messages me and says, "Got a sec?" and I respond, "Sure, I have lots of secs." That's why I keep having children; that's why I have brain damage; and that's why I say the most idiotic things. It's a big circle.

I do occasionally have a logical thought. After negotiating several property disputes, we started marking duplicate toys with the initial of each child. Pick up a random plastic bug, stuffed animal, bottle of water, toothbrush, or chair in our house and you will see the underside or tag labeled with an "A" or "E." This works so well that I'm thinking of creating a Laverne style "L" to put on all MY stuff (the bed, the car radio, the TV) so when arguments arise I can point to the letter and say, "LOOK. THIS IS MINE."

In Conclusion: The Parade of Days

The measurement of time is complex and its analysis spans the entire history of man. Children get a rudimentary exposure to the basics: 7 days in a week, 52 weeks in a year, and so on. As we age, it becomes more apparent that truly every minute counts. So why, then, can we only remember glimmers of moments from our past?

A person in their early thirties will have lived approximately eleven thousand to twelve thousand days. I'd challenge anyone in this age bracket to vividly remember twenty days in his or her life. Diaries suddenly don't seem so silly anymore.

Specific dates also start to gain importance as we age. For instance, I lived my whole life without feeling anything special on a certain day in the fall. And then suddenly it became my firstborn's birthday. This date will now have significant importance in my life and in those of her grandparents and my grandkids. Yet I lived my whole life and never felt a premonition that I'd be in labor during the early hours of that Sunday morning.

When someone important in our life dies, we look back and wonder if we ever felt odd vibes on that day in the past. When my sister hugged her godmother at her wedding, was there a forewarning that the godmother would die that same day sixteen years later? When Tim's aunt congratulated a friend for being pregnant, did she have a quiet intuition that she would be interred the same day the baby was born? We celebrate every New Year rarely considering whether this will be the year that someone important leaves our lives.

These thoughts are staggering and difficult to comprehend. So quit thinking about it and go make each day count.

Appreciate the good and bad that is Your Life's unique Cast of Characters and Parade of Days. And for heaven's sake, don't take things too seriously. Laughter is highly recommended for making longevity tolerable!

www.ingramcontent.com/pod-product-compliance
Lightning Source LLC
Chambersburg PA
CBHW071818020426
42331CB00007B/1530